Edward F. Bayer's Best Poems

EDWARD F. BAYER

Order this book online at www.trafford.com
or email orders@trafford.com

Most Trafford titles are also available at major online book retailers.

Print information available on the last page.

ISBN: 978-1-4907-9306-1 (sc)
ISBN: 978-1-4907-9313-9 (e)

Trafford rev. 03/21/2019

www.trafford.com

North America & international
toll-free: 1 888 232 4444 (USA & Canada)
fax: 812 355 4082

Contents

Utility Bills

by Edward F. Bayer

I am sure in your life;
I am sure in your lifetime;
You have paid utility bills.

Such as gas, electric, telephone;
Water, cable and satellite,
I wish I could say goodnight.

Those utility bills.
Could make us sick;
And we take our pills.

No, not one, not anyone
Could live without them,
Go ahead, take your pills.
But, remember that it is;
Very important to say;
Our utility bills.

The Balk

by Edward F. Bayer

The Pitcher committed the Balk.
The baserunner took a walk
Did the teacher write with the chalk?
It is time that you and I had a talk,
It is best not to waste time and walk.

Please, let the lady talk.
I wrote on the blackboard with the chalk,
I took a nice walk,
I did commit the balk.

The Bore From Baltimore

by Edward F. Bayer

There once was a bore,
Who lived in the city of Baltimore,
Lady, I can love you more,
It is time that I make the store.

The golfer telled fore,
Do not you dare rob the store!
Lady, can you love me more?
The bore was not really;
After all, the bore from Baltimore.

My Life and Lifetime

by Edward F. Bayer

In my life and lifetime;
I have seen many of a crime,
I have had to work and earn a dime,
I have enjoyed drink of lemon and lime,
over the years, I have watched the news.

Yes, it did give me the blues,
At time, I have had the stress,
Too bad, that I am not a member of the press,
Yes, I have been a spelling champion,
As well as being a member of the
International Poetry Hall of Fame.

Too bad, I did not go to Notre Dame,
There were at times when I was down and out,
No, I did not quit nor pout,
No, I did not show strife or time,
I stayed tough, rough, ready and steady,
In my life and lifetime.

The Duel

by Edward F. Bayer

Many at a time and many in history,
People have fought the duel,
The one that lost had to die,
What I say to that is;
O me O my

How time does fly,
Unfortunately, someone had to go,
Too bad, they could not workout their differences,
My heart does grieve;
Because someone had to die.

My dear friends, life should not and must not;
Be like this, this way;
A heart to heart talk;
With each other would have helped;
In order to prevent and stop;
Many of the duel.

On the Boulevard

by Edward F. Bayer

I once travelled on this Boulevard;

It seemed so very hard;

I know at the store I bought some lard;

I also bought some swisshard;

In this board game, I drew this card;

The card said, "Travel on the Boulevard".

The Link

by Edward F. Bayer

The link showed that I was a wanted man;
The link, I thought was not pink but a fink;
They accused me of things I did not do;
If they arrest me, I know I will sue;
They will be bankrupt and blue;
For not being true.

The link will turn pink;
They have their clothes smeared with ink;
Too bad that they will end up in a rink;
The pink, the ink, the rink,
Will all take care of the link.

The Punk

by Edward F. Bayer

There once was the punk;
His head and heart was full of lunk;
He always got into trouble;
The army drill sergeant said "On the double";
He also got in trouble with the law;
Yes, he did turn raw.
Finally, he snapped out of it.

He became a born again Christian;
He accepted Jesus as his personal Lord and savior;
He never did wrong that got him into trouble anymore;
His head and heart was no longer full of lunk.
He was respected and well known;
As a citizen, he was not anymore the Punk.

The Fast Buck

by Edward F. Bayer

There was a criminal who tried to make the Fast Buck;
He tried to change everyone's luck;
His foot got stuck;
He tried to make a fast dollar;
He certainly made people mad and holler;
No, his mind did not rest;

Yes, he was always a pest;
of course, everyone knew that best;
He went to jail;
Of course, nobody paid his bail;
Funny, but not so funny.
His first name truthfully was Buck;
Buck did run out of luck;
Because he tried to make the fast buck.

Be Careful What You Say

by Edward F. Bayer

I am sure in your life;
I am sure in your lifetime;
You have heard the phrase;
Or the expression.

"Be careful what you say"
You may not make someone's day.
Yes, it is time to pray;
Let us talk on the way;
May we stop at the bay;
Be careful what you say.

The Roses

by Edward F. Bayer

The roses yellow, red and white;
Had matches against each other this night;
Yellow rose beat Red rose;
White rose beat Yellow rose;
Red rose beat White rose;
The rose is a great flower.

Be careful not to abuse your power;
I, now have to take my shower;
I enjoy and I am sure everyone else;
Likes to smell with their noses;
The great smell of the roses.

Your Guess is as Good as Mine

by Edward F. Bayer

I am sure in your life;
I am sure in your lifetime;
You probably heard the saying;
Or the phrase known as;
Or your guess is as good as mine.

Many times I have walked the line;
Lady, with that swimsuit you are looking so fine;
Time for me to clean with the chemical of pine;
With that summons you will pay the fine;
Would you please stay in line?
Lady, your guess is as good as mine.

The Roughneck

by Edward F. Bayer

Once upon a time;
There was this guy called "The Roughneck";
He also was know as "Top Fist";
He was also called "The Legend of a Lion";
The Roughneck was rough and tough;

He can break anyone's jaw;
His heart was so raw;
He could not tell a bushel from a peck;
He could not tell if a sandwich was Beefonweck;
He always said "What the Heck".
He got into this fight with guy name Jack.

Jack taught him a lesson to learn;
After Jack beat him up;
Jack and the roughneck became friends;
He was no longer "The Roughneck";
He became "The easy and soft neck";
Now he could tell a bushel from a peck;
His favorite sandwich was Beefonweck;
He no longer said "What the heck";
He was formerly know as "The Roughneck".

The Weed vs. The Flower

by Edward F. Bayer

Many years ago as a young boy;
I remember watching a cartoon;
Focused "The weed vs. the flower".

In real life, weeds have killed flowers;
This was a special exception;
The weed was mean and vicious;
The flower was lovely and sweet;
The cartoon character was trying to make sure;
That the weed would not hurt nor harm the flower;
He would do everything in his power;

He would get a certain spray poison to kill the weed;
That is all he did need;
Always remember, never, ever abuse your power;
I have just told the story the weed vs. the flower.

I will help out

by Edward F. Bayer

Yes, I will help out;
Is this the opening bout?
Lady, you do not have to pout;
Let us give a cheerful shout;
You sure did pout;
Yes, this is the opening bout;
Of course, I will help out.

Teach and Learn

by Edward F. Bayer

All of us teach and learn;
Let me teach and have that peach;
Let me learn so I can earn;
Is it so hard?
Let me have that lard;
Is it easy?
Do not be so sneezie;
Let me learn so I can earn;
Let me teach and have that peach;
Yes, all of us teach and learn.

Knock On Wood

by Edward F. Bayer

I am sure in your life;
I am sure in your lifetime;
You may have heard the expression or phrase;
Known as "Knock on wood";

I hope that you are good;
wood on knock;
I hope you see the clock;
Those birds are a feather flock;
Is this a shock?
This is certainly knock on wood.

The Sleep

by Edward F. Bayer

This was known as the sleep;

My dream was weep;

I did hear a beep;

Remember "Nellybelle", Pat Brady's Jeep?;

Please do not weep;

Yes, this was the sleep;

"zzzzzzzzzzzzzzzz".

The Fork From New York

by Edward F. Bayer

This is the fork from New York;
This is the York of New;
Is this the York of the Fork?
Is it the Fork of the Stork?
The York of New of the dew;
It is time for that beef stew;
It is time for that Fork;
The Fork from New York.

The Stun

by Edward F. Bayer

I have just received the stun;
I have received shocking news;
It has certainly gave me the blues;
This stun was news about the sun;
Will the sun be done?
Will this news be the only one?
This news was known as "The Stun".

The No-Show

by Edward F. Bayer

Some years ago, my old high school;
Had a 25 year reunion;
I decided not to go;
I was known as "The No-Show";
The reason was those girls;
In that class of years ago;
Did not want me;

I was and I still am going out with someone;
They did not want me then;
They cannot have me now;
So I say to them;
"Aw, Poor baby";
I was glad as hell to be known as, "The No-Show".

My Two Cares

by Edward F. Bayer

In my life and in my lifetime;
My two cares or two things that I care about;
They are respect for life and not abusing one's power;

Are you about to take your shower?
Please do not pout.
I wonder what this is all about.
Do not pout the power
Do not power the pout;
I say to you, please eat your pears;
I love you, all, but please understand;
My two cares.

Steady Eddie

by Edward F. Bayer

Just about all my friends;
Call me "Steady Eddie".
Touch and steady;
Rough and ready;
Is Eddie steady?
Eddie is not rough;
Eddie is not tough;
It certainly tickles me pink;
To be known and called "Steady Eddie".

Stumped

by Edward F. Bayer

The champ finally got stumped;
The newcomer got him trumped;
The champ could not take the heat;
The champ knew he was finally beat;

He was mad;
Later he was sad;
The newcomer was so glad;
The audience was singing;
"Na, na, na, na, na, na"
"Hey, hey, hey, good-bye;
To the beaten champ;
After all the champ finally got stumped.

The Pink Slip

by Edward F. Bayer

The boss handed the employee;
The pink slip;
He knew he was fired from his job;
He told the boss that he was wrong;
It made the boss's day long;
After that the boss did not know what to say;
The boss realized he made a mistake;

His employee gave him no lip;
When he told him that he was wrong;
The employee told his boss;
To go jump in the lake;
"You were the one to make this mistake"; he said to him,
"I never gave you any lip"
"You were the one that gave me the pink slip".

It Is Wrong To Drink And Take Drugs

by Edward F. Bayer

It is wrong to drink.
It is wrong to take drugs.
You will soon be in ink.
You will be jail thugs.

It will take away your freedom.
It will take away your clean mind.
You are the only one I could find.
It will take away your driver's license.
You may never be able to drive again.

A word to the wise;
Never, ever spit in the air;
Because it will come right back;
Be smart and be wise;
It is wrong to drink and take drugs.

Claim Jumping And Murder

by Edward F. Bayer

In one of the Lone Ranger episodes;
Two young men were arrested;
For claim jumping and murder
They were both brothers in this story;
They were totally innocent;
They were falsely accused;
This man who killed his partner;
Had them arrested by the sheriff;
The Lone Ranger and Tonto figured it all out;
That the killer had his reasons to pout;
His motives was to kill his partner;
And to claim the silver that the brothers had found;
The Lone Ranger captured him as the story ended.

The Hot Child

by Edward F. Bayer

This young girl was known;
As the hot child;
She sure was wild;
She left school early as sixteen;
She wanted to have sex with everyman;
She did not care whether he was married or not;
All the married men told her no;
Most of the single men told her no;
Some of them said yes;
But then moved on with their lives;
She got herself in trouble with the law;
Her life turned raw;
She was let go with a warning;
She later became a policewoman;
She was no longer wild;
She was no longer the hot child.

My Lips Are Sealed

by Edward F. Bayer

I am sure in your life;
I am sure in your lifetime;
You have heard the phrase or saying;
"My lips are sealed"
Information cannot and will not be revealed;
I have not anything to say;
It may ruin someone's day;
I cannot and will not accept a bribe;
It will not transcribe;
It will not be revealed;
I tell you that my lips are sealed.

I Want To Be A Humble Servant In Our Lord

by Edward F. Bayer

I am not better than you,
I am not better than anyone else,
No, I am not better that your neighbor,
No, I am not better than my neighbors,
I wan to be a humble servant in the our Lord.

This is all one accord,
I can and will smile,
I will try to love all,
Yes, this world is very small,
Let us abide with each other,
Let us all work with each other.

Let us enjoy one another,
This is a command accord,
I want to be a humble servant in our Lord.

A Long Time Ago

by Edward F. Bayer

A long time ago, I had a choice to make,
No it was not a fake.
It was a decision to make and it was,
About going to my 25-year high school reunion and I
did not go.

Yes, I had my reasons and I stayed away,
I gave them a chance to go out,
with me back then,
They told me no
Now they want me,
I do not want them.

I am already going out with someone new,
They had their way,
Now they must pay,
They had a chance to go,
A long time ago.

I Love Attention

by Edward F. Bayer

I love attention
I always love to be "The Main Event",
I always want to be "The Main Attraction",
I do not want to be a subtraction,
My fun needs to be an addition, plus a main
multiplication.

There must not be any division,
I will try to keep everyone united as one,
I must and should, of course have my private life,
So there is no strife,
I must defend my life,
Watch out for multiplication, division, addition, and
subtraction.
I love attention.

The Message

by Edward F. Bayer

I was asked to take the message,

A message from one very important person,

To another important person,

Everyone was told to stay out of my way,

I had to also deliver those replies,

This way there would not be any lies,

I was asked to judge all of these pies,

I judge with respect and fairness,

Yes, It did make my day,

Because everyone stayed out of the way,

As I did carry the message.

The Tumble

by Edward F. Bayer

Yes, I took a terrific tumble,
I began to rumble,
Yes, it did make me humble,
I took a good fall,
As I caught that ball,
I ran as hard and fast as I could.
You knew that I would.

Yes, I did answer the call,
I knew that, great skill and all,
It did make me humble,
That was a loud rumble,
I had to unfortunately take the tumble.

I Rank With The Best

by Edward F. Bayer

I truthfully hate to brag,
The dog has his own tail to wag,
I rank with the best,
The best of poems and poetry,
Yes, I am in the International Poetry Hall of Fame,
Yes, I do play many of a board game,
Yes I am a life time member of the International Society
of Poets,
If you do not like what I say,
"I say to you, aw poor baby,"
From North to South,
From East to West,
I rank with the best.

Aw, Poor Baby!

by Edward F. Bayer

I said to my losing opponent,
"Aw, Poor baby"
You will do better next time,
Did you find that dime?
Do not take that lime,
Why would I commit a crime?
My opponent beat me in the rematch,
That opponent said to me,
"Aw, Poor baby!"

The Boomerang

by Edward F. Bayer

This curving hook stick was known,
As the boomerang,
This thing did hang,
It looked like a U.F.O.
It did say no,
It hooked, glide and slide

All of us had to keep our cool,
I finally saw it coming
I lifted my hand and caught it.
It did rang,
It always had a bang,
Yes, it did hang,
This was known as the boomerang.

The Surprise

by Edward F. Bayer

All of us had the surprise,

For someone we knew,

I planned this secret,

I told my closest friends,

They all agreed with me,

This was a surprise birthday party,

This never came so hardy,

This person was so surprised,

This person did not know what to say,

This was to make his day,

The sun did rise,

This was known as the surprise.

A Humble Servant In Our Lord

by Edward F. Bayer

A humble servant in our Lord,

Is not better than anyone else,

That person respects and protects human life,

Does not and will not show any strife,

That person does not and will not gossip,

That person will show a smile,

That person will share a laugh,

That human being will always show,

A christian love and respect for all,

That is a humble servant in our Lord.

The Delight

by Edward F. Bayer

This was known as the delight,
Of course, you are very right,
I did see the light,
He did hit the ball with all his might,
What a great sight,
Yes, this was the delight.

The Debate

by Edward F. Bayer

These number of politicians had "The Debate",
In quest of their party's nomination,
They had no combination,
They were in different variation,
No, I did not tell the name of their party,
Am I sure you remember this only name Hardy,
It was so late,
Make sure you love and not hate,
Are you sure this is the debate?

The Stronghold

by Edward F. Bayer

This wrestler had this other wrestler,
In "The Stronghold",
This hold of strong,
Went very long,
The crowd began to cheer his name,
He was soon in pro wrestling's hall of fame,
He wore many championship belts of gold,
He was very bold,
He was known as the stronghold.

The Hub Of A Tub

by Edward F. Bayer

This was known as the hub of a tub,
Does this mean you bub,
I drank the glub,
Would you like to join this club?
This is also the tub of a hub,
Stop drinking you glub,
Yes, I was the bub,
He was known as the hub of a tub.

Into The Day

by Edward F. Bayer

We left for our trip into the day,
The day was gray,
Our fishing trip was down at the bay,
I had to cash my check first at the bank,

No, my name is not Frank,
Is his name Hank?
Please fill up my gas tank,
We finally arrived at the bay,
The day was still gray,
It is twelve noon into the day.

Make That Turn

by Edward F. Bayer

I ordered the taxi-cab driver;

Make that turn,

Did you see that hours burn?

Am I going to churn?

No, there will not be any concern,

There was a discern,

It is now time for you to make that turn.

The Arrest

by Edward F. Bayer

The police, the sheriff, state police,
The F.B.I. as well as myself,
All of us teamed up to make the arrest,
All of them, gave me jurisdiction power;
As well as authority to lead this posse,

This drug dealing became a pest,
My information to the authorities, were the very best,
We eliminated this pest,
Yes, This was known as the arrest.

New Broom And Newsweep

by Edward F. Bayer

I am sure in your life,
I am sure in your lifetime,
You have heard of the expression,
Or you heard the phrase known,
As "Newbroom and Newsweep",

This is a fact of life when,
A new boss or a new politician,
Takes control,
You may or you may not like it,
If you do not like it,

I say to you "Oh, poor baby",
This is the way when it comes to newbroom and
newsweep.

We Need Mary More Lone Rangers

by Edward F. Bayer

In this world today,
In this life today,
We need many more Lone Rangers,
To protect our homeland,
To fight the war on terrorism,
To fight all crimes and wrongdoings,
To establish justice, law and order,
To establish peace, truth and reasoning,
To fight the war in Iraq,
We do not need strangers,
We need many more Lone Rangers.

Are We On The Same Page?

by Edward F. Bayer

Are we on the same page?
I need to know your age,
You do not have to be a road rage,
Do you do your acts on a stage,
This person has caused a rage,
Please, do not tell me your age,
Are we on the same page?

The Pet Shop II

by Edward F. Bayer

This is know as the petshop II,
I wonder if the dog, that beagle,
That looked like my dog King was still there,
I was to open the door,
As I made my way in,

I did look and there was a dog that looked like
Rintintin, a German shepherd.
There was a collie dog that looked like Lassie,
There was a black and white cat that looked a lot like my
cat Tommy, years before King,
As he was a beagle hound dog.

I asked that store clerk if that was the same dog,
He said "The Dog that you saw last time"
"Was sold to a family",
He also said "This is a female relative of my dog",
"Her name is "Fudgie",
It was so nice to see another dog that looked like my dog
King.

The Fraud

by Edward F. Bayer

There was once "The Fraud",
Who caused a lot of trouble,
This person committed a felony,
This beyond doubt was a serious crime,
This person lied and covered up,
Many more lies,
Jumped many claims,
Stoled many of a gold,
This was a story to be told,
He committed "The Fraud".

What Do You Mean?

by Edward F. Bayer

What do you mean?
My sugar Jelly bean,
Is this cooked meat,
Or is it lean and tough?
Like a rough, tough cream puff,
Are you lean and rough?
Are you mean and tough?
Is this bean lean?
Is this the lean and bean?
Tell me, what do you mean?

Have Game Will Travel

by Edward F. Bayer

I am have game will travel,
I travel to many places challenging,
Anybody and everybody to games,
such as checkes, chess and mancala, hijara and tote,
All people take note.

That I like to play partners as teams,
I have several partners and more,
With the game of sequence and sequence dice,
Life is not a bore,
For have game will travel.

The Garbage Pickers Club

by Edward F. Bayer

People at times drive by,
And look for garbage on the road,
They pick up things that they want,
or things that they need,
This is called the garbage pickers club,
This club is absolutely free,

There is not any price for this club,
It is true that someone's trash,
Does become somebody's treasure,
It has many a pleasure,
No cash for this trash,
What do you say, Bub?
Join the garbage pickers club.

The Name Of The Game

by Edward F. Bayer

This is the name of the game,
Does this game have a name?
Does the name have a game?
Just like me, are you in any hall of fame,
Is this all the same?
Are you another flame?
That poor horse went lame,
Am I the blame?
This is the name of the game.

The Divide

by Edward F. Bayer

The three of us,
The Lone Ranger, Roy Rogers and Yours Truly,
Cowboy Joe took a ride on the divide,
All of us were looking for one of the most vicious gangs
of the West.

All of them were a pest,
All the sheriffs and marshalls,
Knew that best,

The three of us got help from a possie,
For all of us together finally put them,
Out of business,
After this was all over,
We rode off of the divide.

Edward F. Bayer

by Edward F. Bayer

My name is Edward F. Bayer
Does anyone care?
My middle initial is F.
That F stands for Francis
I do have many likes
Yes, I do have many dislikes.

I am not trying to brag
The dog has its own tail to wag
I am not the greatest guy in the world
I am not better than anyone else nor you
I am just like a rock standing still
It is time to take my vitamin pill.

Is anyone out there conscientious?
Will anyone care?
Ladies and gentlemen
My name is Edward F. Bayer.

It Makes Me Feel Good

by Edward F. Bayer

It makes me feel good;
When we challenge each other in games
For example:
Jolene challenged Teresa
I challenged Jolene
Teresa challenged me
It has posed a challenge to a survey at sea
I wish I could say
Did this make your day?
You knew that it would
This 3 way challenge, It makes me feel good.

The Secret Files

by Edward F. Bayer

There was once a secret firm
That had the secret files
I cannot tell the name of the firm
Because of privacy and confidentiality
These secret files had miles long
Sometimes these files were dead wrong
I have to go where I belong
Yes, there were miles of files
It did make many piles
They were known as the secret files.

A Scream In The Dark

by Edward F. Bayer

I heard a scream in the dark
It was late at night
It was around midnight
Midnight is called "The witch's hour"
My friend, the bird, the dark lark;
Could not tell me what it was

I had to get a posse of men
Together for thy very important mission
We had to figure out this situation
When we found out that it was a murder
We looked to see who to arrest
All of us knew who the guilty person was
We arrested a woman on a suspicion of murder
As well as claim jumping
Yes, it was a dark cold night
As I heard a scream in the dark.

We Have Each Other Opposed

by Edward F. Bayer

We have each other opposed
This is to be supposed
Opposed to be supposed
Supposed to be opposed
You knew that this would
This makes me feel good
Judy opposed Betty
I opposed Judy
Betty opposed me
How could this all be?
This is to be supposed
We have each other opposed

Red Tape

by Edward F. Bayer

I am sure in your life
I am sure in your lifetime
You have heard of those words called, red tape
Is it really red tape?
May I see this ape?
Do not touch this grape
The tape is definitely red
Is his name Ted?
Lady, I am now going to put you to bed
Hey girl, watch out for led
Who wants a black sled?
Watch out for a led of the sled
That not anyone of us is a grape
Is it too late for red tape?

Friend Or Foe

by Edward F. Bayer

Are you my friend or foe?
I need to know
Are you in my side or not?
Do not tie yourself in a knot
If you are not friend nor foe
Look like it as even if
You do not know me
To a swim as the sea
This is something that you must know
Either I do know you or not
Or are you my friend or foe?

Hello!?

by Edward F. Bayer

A coach said to his pro football team
After starting the season with a 1-win lost-6 record
One of the words in a peptalk to
His team was hello!!
Did his team have them Jello?
Did they learn the game Othello?
Did they all sing "O me O mio?
They turned it around
They got out of a jam
They got with the program
They woke up
I wonder if they had their 7-up
Anyone want to play me in Othello?
Can anyone sing "O me o Mio?
Please let me eat my Jello!
I say to you all "Hello!!"

I Almost Got Put Away

by Edward F. Bayer

Once upon a time
This is a true story
I take not any glory
I almost got put away
This is what I was told
I can be very bold
If I was put away
I would have banned and barred
All visitors from seeing me
I could have been null and void
What I am today
The person that told me "I almost put you away is no
longer around"
No, I do not hold any grudges
I thank God that
I was not put away.

Hot Dog Heaven

by Edward F. Bayer

There is a hot dog stand
The name of it is "Hot Dog Heaven"
Loads of people come in there everyday
I know the owner and manger well
This is a great story to tell
No, I cannot go with you to the bay
Unfortunately, you with the dice, did not roll a seven
The name of the place is "Hot Dog Heaven"

Seneca Texas Red Hots

by Edward F. Bayer

There is a hot dog stand
The name of it is "Seneca Texas Red Hots"
The place has you tied in knots
I know the manager well
This is clearly as sold as a bell

The Can Of Oil

by Edward F. Bayer

The can of oil did not spoil
This had a load of top soil
All this did not last
This was going to be in the past
This all happened very fast
This soil did not spoil
This was the can of oil.

Too Bad For You

by Edward F. Bayer

Too bad for you

Now you are just like cooked stew

You are a total waste

You are just like tomato paste

You are nothing but a crumb

I know that you are dumb

You are now cooked stew

Too bad for you

Free To Be Born

by Edward F. Bayer

We are free to be born
Please be quiet and eat your corn
This is a bright September morn

This is a bright sunny morn
Please for the thousandth time, eat your corn
By golly, we are free to be born

The Blackout

by Edward F. Bayer

There once was the blackout
Nor power nor electricity
This blackout was caused by an ice storm
This was one of the worst in history

It took about one week to get back to power
Now everyone can take their shower
It started at the witch's hour
Soon everyone starred to pout
What caused the blackout?

True Blue

by Edward F. Bayer

Do you know that I am the true blue?
True is always blue
Blue is always true
So, what else is new?

Make sure you eat your beef stew
Did you see that ball that she threw?
I already ate my beef stew
Yes, I know that person is new
Is true blue?
Is blue true?
Make sure that you are true blue

A Song In The Air

by Edward F. Bayer

I always have a song in the air
I always love to sing
I play some musical instruments too
I love to be the entertainer
I just love doing a show
So people get to know
That this bird has a wing
I always just do not despair
I always have a song in the air

The Mind Is A Terrible Thing To Waste

by Edward F. Bayer

I am sure in your life
In your lifetime
You may have heard and seen an Ad
In our television and radio
"The mind is a terrible thing to waste"
Going to school and being given a tool
Following the golden rule
When behaving in a corner on a stool
Learning in school
Having a story to tell
Tell it very well
Can you hear the bell?
Let us make tomato paste
The mind is a terrible thing to waste

The Stars Are Out Tonight

by Edward F. Bayer

The stars are out tonight
They shine so bright
Mister, you have got that right
Oh, what a gorgeous sight
It is a moonless night
Starlight, star bright, I see tonight
It is again, a moonless night
Oh, what a brilliant sight
Lady, you are so right
The stars shine so bright
The stars are out tonight

The Emotion

by Edward F. Bayer

Many years ago, I stood before
An audience in my senior year
In high school
This was my last basketball game at home
Which was also our last game of these
I was the first of six seniors introduced
"Number 35, Eddie Bayer"
I showed no emotion that was the emotion
All the fans and students were there
The emotion was that I did not care
No, I did not cry nor did I despair
Yes, they gave me a cheer
No, I was never queer
It's now time for my tan lotion
This was a true story
No emotion was the emotion

The Spin

by Edward F. Bayer

At one time there was the spin

I wonder if I did win

Can you put on this pin?

I cannot believe I saw your twin

Is this steel or tin?

Lady, it is time for you to pack it in

If you lie, it is a sin

I will not pack it in

I told you before, it is tin

Nyah, nyah, I saw your twin

I do not want this pin

Who cares, If I did win

This is too fast for the spin

At This Stage Of The Game

by Edward F. Bayer

I am sure in your life
And in your lifetime
You have heard the expression or phrase
At this stage of the game
Is there anybody besides me
In poetry's hall of fame?
What is your name?
I do not have anyone to blame
Am I fire or some other flame?
My dog King's foot went lame
I love you just the same
It is too early to tell
At this stage of the game

The March

by Edward F. Bayer

There once was the march
The march went from Houston to Miami
No, this march was not full of salami
All of us had to sweat
We had sweat, blood and tears
We did not get any cheers
None of us stopped for any beers
At the end this, I will get you yet
Spaghetti, macaroni and bread are starch
Yes, I remember this was the march

I Live Alone

by Edward F. Bayer

Yes it is true that I live alone
I do have a telephone
No, I cannot throw that stone
It may hurt someone's bone
I do live a lonely life
I can not show strife
I can not throw this knife
I still wish I had my dog King
When he passed away it hurt like a sting
I wished at times someone would give me a ring
I will not throw this knife
I will not show strife
Of course, I live a lonely life
I will not hurt anyone's bone
No I will not throw that stone
Please call me on my telephone
Yes, it is true that I live alone

The Instigator

by Edward F. Bayer

Once upon a time there was the Instigator
He caused trouble wherever he went
He was an impostor
He was a liar
He was a cheat
He was a thief
He also was a murderer
He also caused marriages to end
He never had a friend
He could never be trusted
He caused many to be busted
He finally got caught
He had his trial
He was sentenced to die in the electric chair
That was the end of the Instigator

Smile Awhile

by Edward F. Bayer

I want to see you smile awhile
No matter how great or how do life is
No matter what the situation is
No matter what the cost
No smile is a lost
A smile is a gain
A smile gives and show no pain
Make sure that smile will last awhile
Always smile awhile

The Off Sound

by Edward F. Bayer

This sure was an off sound
Where was it bound
Was it from my dog King, who is a beagle hound
Could it be from lost and found
Is it from the pitcher's mound?
It may be from lost and found
It is not from King my dog beagle hound
I know where it was bound
There went the off sound.

Aim To Please

by Edward F. Bayer

I am sure in your life
I am sure in your lifetime
You may have heard the expression phrase
Known as "Aim to Please"
Did this person want this piece of cheese?
Is she enjoying the tropical breeze?
Lady I love you, but do not squeeze
I am of course, enjoying this breeze
I would like this piece of cheese
All of us always aim to please.

The Tattle Tale

by Edward F. Bayer

Their once was a person
This particular person was known and called, The Tattle Tale
This person also drank a lot of ale
Who lived on a street called "stale"
this person's skin was very pale
Never, ever got any mail
This person could go to jail
For killing this bird called "Quail"
This person had a big mouth
This person lived in the South
That bird was called a quail
That person went to jail
That person never had any mail
I was splashed by a water pail
My skin was supposedly stale
I never drank any ale
She was known as the Tattle Tale.

The Sun Tan

by Edward F. Bayer

There once was a woman very young
She got herself "The Sun Tan"
She forgot the sun tan lotion
She was all emotion
It was so hot
You could cook soup outside in the pot
The sun was loved an awful lot
Her skin was badly burned
It was enough to make it turned
So, my dear friends, make this a lesson
And a lesson well learned
Always use a sun tan lotion
Take no emotion
Do not be like a frying pan
Make sure you get the true sun tan.

The Magic Lamp

by Edward F. Bayer

There was once a magic lamp
It had a golden stamp
Did this genie come from a camp?
Watch out for that vamp
Did you see me slide down the ramp?
I see that vamp
I have been to a camp
Time for you to receive your stamp
There was once a magic lamp.

Rise And Shine

by Edward F. Bayer

In our lives and in our lifetime
Each and everyday we have to rise and share
Whether it is getting up and going to work
Whether it is going to school
Whether it is going to Sunday's school or church
Or it may be doing our daily chores
Like it or not, rise and shine.

The Dark Lark

by Edward F. Bayer

The dark lark always flew at night
The eagle, hawk and falcon
Was on this bird's trail
These three birds were a posse
The dark lark was an innocent bird
It was telling the trust of word
It never hurt a humble being nor animal, nor a bird
It was like a fugitive on a run
It never had any fun
That bird was trying to reach his family
Some human killed off those that
Were looking for him
And finally that bird was able to return home
This was the story of the dark lark.

At The Camp Again

by Edward F. Bayer

I was invited back to this camp
Both Betty the lifeguard
And Barbara the nurse were both happy to see me
This time the nurse and lifeguard, switched swimsuits
The nurse Barbara wore a one piece
swimsuit, while Betty this time wore a bikini swimsuit
We got to continue our rivalry in
Our games of checkers against each other
This time it was a horse of a different color
Betty beat Barbara
I beat Betty
Barbara beat me
It seems to me all of us never had enough of each other
Of course, all of us had games with each other
Of course, I got to meet new people
I got to be at the camp again.

Sock'em Swato

by Edward F. Bayer

When I was a young boy
From 5-10 years of age
I used to say when I watch a western on television I used
to say "Sock'em swato"
The Lone Rangers sidekick was Tonto
Lady, are you from Toronto?
Are you on the bio?
O me O mio!
Yes, I have been to Toronto
It was challenge for Tonto
Can you hear me say, "sock'em swato?

The Drill

by Edward F. Bayer

The army did the drill

Is this pickle a dill?

I am not that ill

It is time to take my pill

Is this guy's name phil?

Make sure you clean up your spill

My name is not Phil

Time to take your pill

Are you ill?

That pickle is a dill

Yes, The army did the drill

The Love Line

by Edward F. Bayer

There once were many women
They were all lined up
Ready to make love to me
This line was called "The love line"
I would meet with each and every lady
From ages 18 and up
Some of them were married
But the majority of them were not
I could not believe this was happening
I could not believe that they were all mine
I was stunned that this was so fine
I just could not believe this was the love line

Plain And Simple

by Edward F. Bayer

Somethings in life are plain and simple
Did you squeeze out that pimple?
Is this color purple?
The color is black
What did you lack?
Did I make that drive?
Try to survive
I squeezed out the pimple
Somethings are plain and simple.

The Wild Card

by Edward F. Bayer

The wild card was a wild card
It was so hard
It was solid as lard
The wild card was a Jack
It took you back
No, my name is not Mack
I did blow my stack
This vamp has made it as lard
Don't be so hard
This was certainly the wild card.

The False Witness

by Edward F. Bayer

There once was the false witness
Who lied under oath in court
Whose testimony could have helped the innocent
The innocent was the accused who was on trial
The false witness later was on trial
For perjury, for lying under oath

A felony was slapped on his criminal record
So my dear friends, always tell the truth
The truth can help the innocent
The truth can and does get the guilty
Never ever be like the false witness

Lady I Am Not Interested In You

by Edward F. Bayer

Lady, I am not interested in you
What makes you think so?
Why are you interested in me?
Is it because of my looks?
Give me some hooks
Is it because of my charms?
I know you would take me in your arms
Is it because of my personality?
Keep it confidentiality
You could try all you want
Lady, you have struck out
I know you are mad and want to pout
Poor baby, you are wasting your time
It is time for me to cook my beef stew
Lady for the thousandth time
Lady, I am not interested in you!!!

Della From Philadelphia

by Edward F. Bayer

There was once a charming lady
She was known as Della from Philadelphia
She was one sweet Della
Great for any one Fella
Her middle name was Stella
Her last name I cannot tell
I know it all too well
Want me to ring the liberty bell?
What do you want me to sell?
Her full name is Della Stella
Look out fella
Yes, her name is Della
She is Della from Philadelphia.

Gorgeous Jo From Toledo

by Edward F. Bayer

From this Northern Ohio City

She come from Toledo

Is gorgeous Jo from Toledo

She weighs 100 pounds and is 5 feet 4

Her built was galore

She was a brunette

He middle name was Claudette

She had a smart personality

She did have congeniality

She had looks so fine

I could not believe she was mine

Her blue lipstick did shine

She was known as gorgeous Jo

She was known as gorgeous Jo from Toledo

Go To Chicago

by Edward F. Bayer

Once upon a time there was a game
The name of the game was "Go to Chicago"
This was something that I did know
It was something that I wanted to show
The game was similar to Monopoly
Too bad, I never took biology
It also had a boardwalk
It caused the Cubs and White Sox pitchers to balk
It caused also, the Bulls and Bears to stalk
This was all about the windy city
The game kept us very busy
All of us did know
The name of the game was "Go to Chicago"

Out Like A Light

by Edward F. Bayer

This boxer was out like a light
This was the end of the fight
He was definitely knocked out
Not anyone did pout
The party is over
I am looking over this four leaf clover
Did you not have a dog named Rover?
Turn off the lights, the party is over
He went to protest and pout
He was positively knocked out
This was a great fight
But the champion was out like a light

We Have Each Other Bested

by Edward F. Bayer

We have each other bested
I am already rested
Bested me as beat
Do not you think that is kind of neat?
The three of us gave each other
A besting whipping
Sandy whipped Jolene
I smacked Sandy
Jolene lambasted me
That was more than a triple tie
That was a whipping slaughter besting
What still made me feel good
Was we played each other
How those two feel, I do not know
It was a great show
This was already tested
We have each other bested.

They Jumped Us

by Edward F. Bayer

On September 11, 2001, they jumped us
Yes, this caused a war on terrorism
Osama Bin Laden and his men did this
We never, ever did anything to them
No, not one, not in the book
They did give us a look
They gave us a terrible hook
This jump was not a checkers game
This jump put us to shame
America still has its name
We were doing good, like a bus
To cause a war, they jumped us.

The Law Is Not Raw

by Edward F. Bayer

The law is not raw
Is raw the law?
May I take that straw?
The crow went
caw, caw, caw"
The Southern boy said "Aw, maw"
Did I say, "Caw, caw caw?"
Hands off of that straw
I am not the law
The law is not raw.

The Land Of Cleveland

by Edward F. Bayer

There is this big industrial city on the Northeast part of
Ohio near lake Erie, and that is Cleveland
The land of Cleveland
Is so big and grand
It has the Indians
I hope they are not on the war path
It has the Browns
I hope they are not clowns
It also has the Cavaliers
I hope they ride well
So, I may know the city swell
So, I may know it grand
The land of Cleveland.

Gigi From Miami

by Edward F. Bayer

From this great city on
The Eastern Florida Coast
Come, Gigi from Miami
She was 5 feet 8 inches tall
Her built was galore
She wore a one piece as well as a bikini
Her name was Gigi
She was Gigi from Miami

Three Ladies In A Polka

by Edward F. Bayer

There were once these three ladies
Who enjoyed dancing a Polish polka with each other
First, there was Sue who wore a bare back black dress
Second, there was Pat who wore a halter top
Floral with a floral long length skirt
Third and last of all, there was Diane who wore a
sleeveless white dress
In the first polka, Diane asked Pat
In the second polka, Sue asked Diane
In the third polka, Pat asked Sue
They got each other to dance
They are three ladies in a polka.

Printed in the United States
By Bookmasters